SELECTED THEMES FROM THE MOTION

HARRY POTTER

AND THE
SORCERER'S STONE

Project Manager: Carol Cuellar
Arranged by: Bill Galliford, Ethan Neuburg and Tod Edmondson
Book Art Layout: Nancy Rehm

Album Cover Artwork © 2001 Warner Bros.

WARNER BROS. PUBLICATIONS
Warner Music Group
An AOL Time Warner Company
USA: 15800 NW 48th Avenue, Miami, FL 33014

WARNER/CHAPPELL MUSIC

CANADA: 15800 N.W. 48th AVENUE
MIAMI, FLORIDA 33014
SCANDINAVIA: P.O. BOX 533, VENDEVAGEN 85 B
S-182 15, DANDERYD, SWEDEN
AUSTRALIA: P.O. BOX 353
3 TALAVERA ROAD, NORTH RYDE N.S.W. 2113
ASIA: THE PENINSULA OFFICE TOWER, 12th FLOOR
18 MIDDLE ROAD
TSIM SHA TSUI, KOWLOON, HONG KONG

Carisch
NUOVA CARISCH

ITALY: VIA CAMPANIA, 12
20098 S. GIULIANO MILANESE (MI)
ZONA INDUSTRIALE SESTO ULTERIANO
SPAIN: MAGALLANES, 25
28015 MADRID
FRANCE: CARISCH MUSICOM,
25, RUE D'HAUTEVILLE, 75010 PARIS

IMP
INTERNATIONAL MUSIC PUBLICATIONS LIMITED

ENGLAND: GRIFFIN HOUSE,
161 HAMMERSMITH ROAD, LONDON W6 8BS
GERMANY: MARSTALLSTR. 8, D-80539 MUNCHEN
DENMARK: DANMUSIK, VOGNMAGERGADE 7
DK 1120 KOBENHAVNK

CONTENTS

DIAGON ALLEY

Music by
JOHN WILLIAMS

Joyously ♩ = 120

Diagon Alley - 3 - 1
0639B

Diagon Alley - 3 - 3
0639B

FAMILY PORTRAIT

Music by
JOHN WILLIAMS

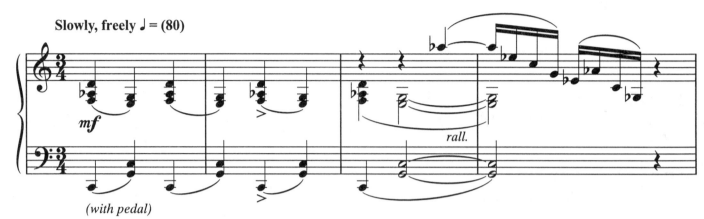

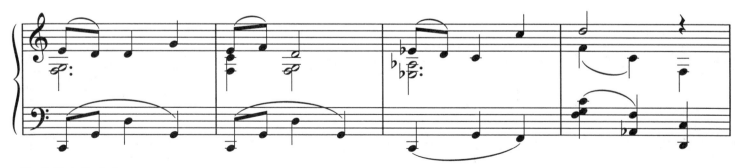

Family Portrait - 4 - 1
0639B

Family Portrait - 4 - 4
0639B

FLUFFY'S HARP

Music by
JOHN WILLIAMS

Witches lullaby—dreamily (♩ = 72)

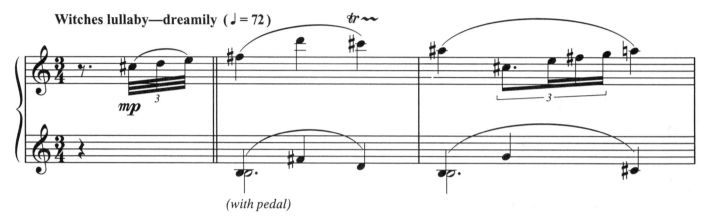

(with pedal)

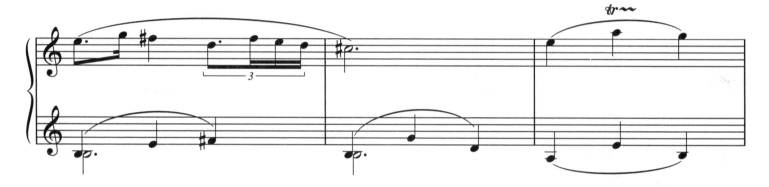

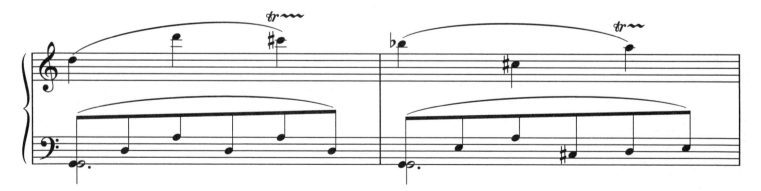

Fluffy's Harp - 4 - 1
0639B

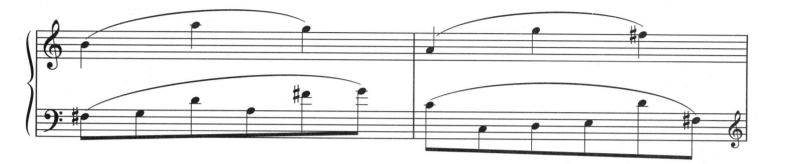

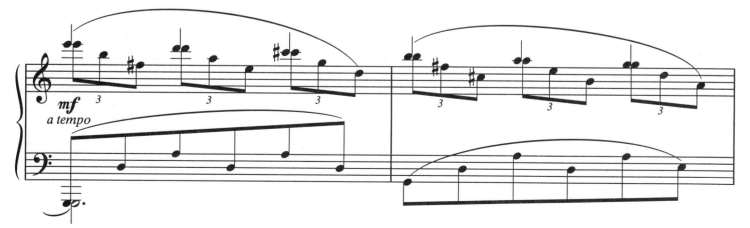

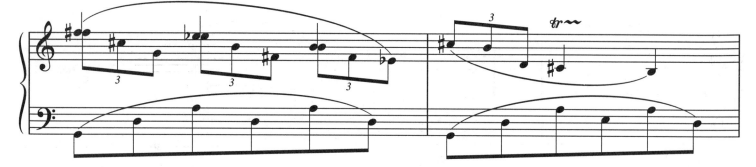

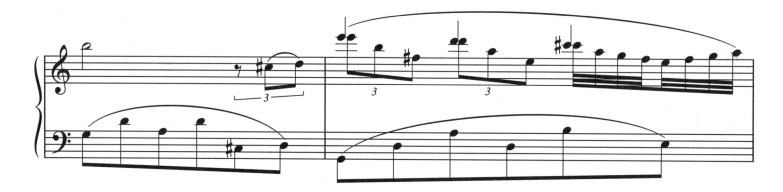

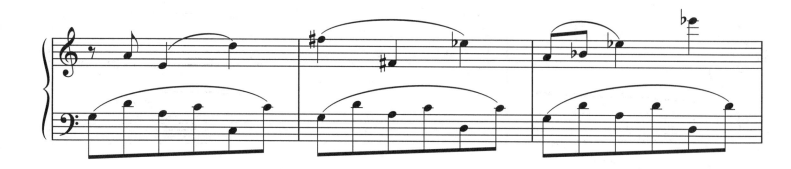

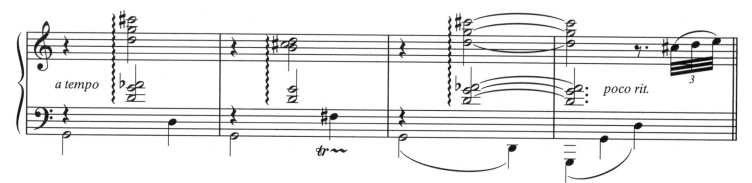

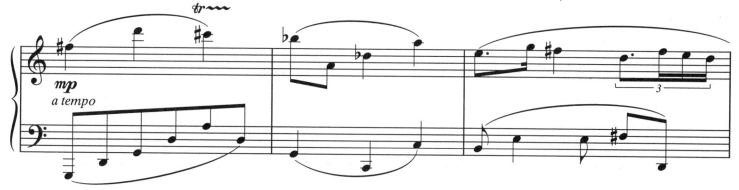

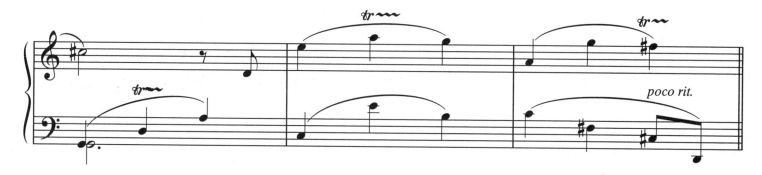

HARRY'S WONDROUS WORLD

Music by
JOHN WILLIAMS

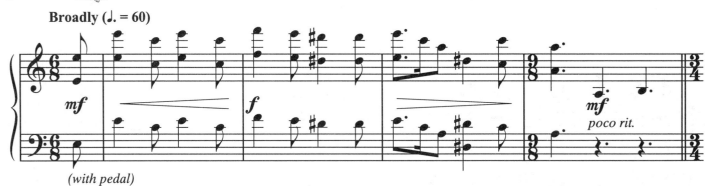

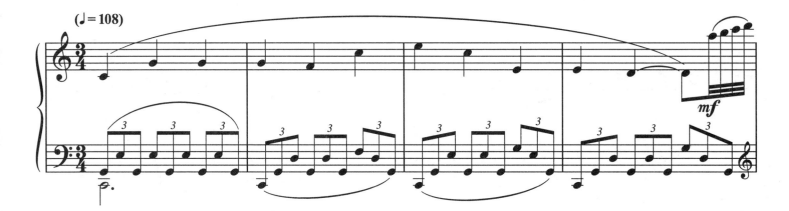

Harry's Wondrous World - 11 - 2
0639B

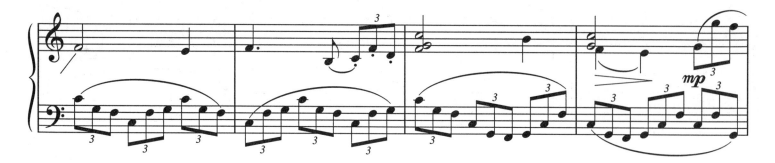

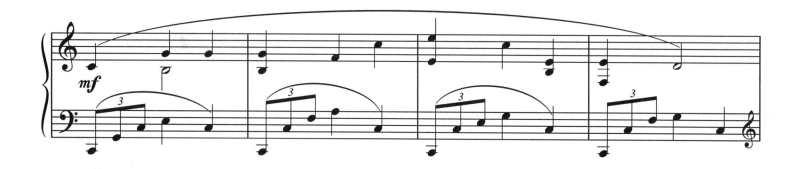

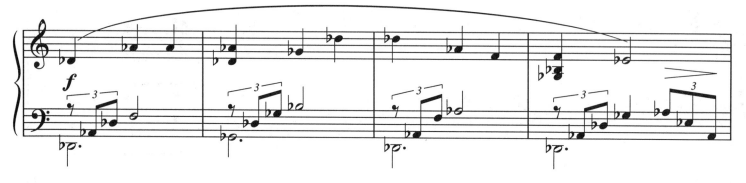

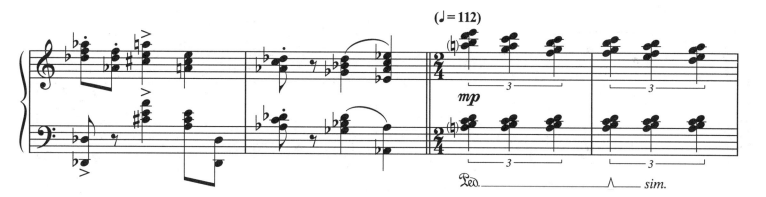

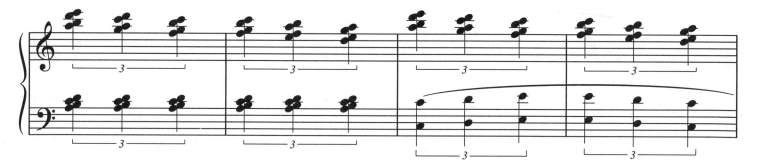

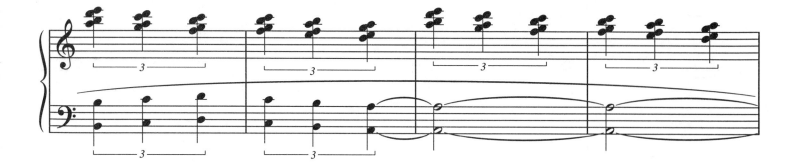

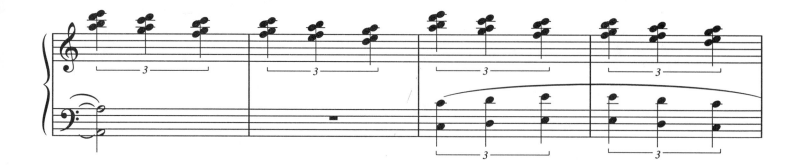

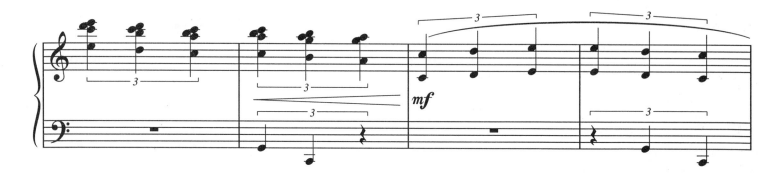

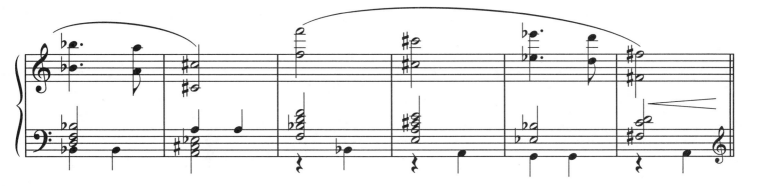

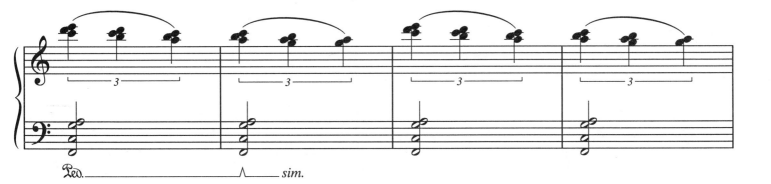

26

(♩. = 120)

Victoriously

Broadly

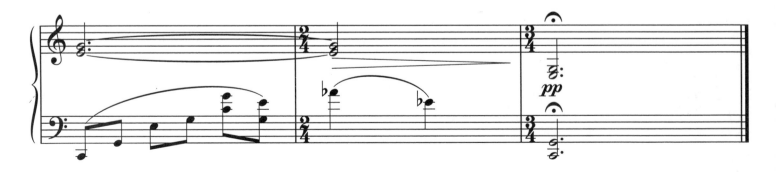

NIMBUS 2000

Music by
JOHN WILLIAMS

Magico ♩ = 80

Nimbus 2000 - 3 - 1
0639B

QUIDDITCH

Music by
JOHN WILLIAMS

Heroically ♩. =120

Quidditch - 3 - 1
0639B

42

Broadly

Quidditch - 3 - 2
0639B

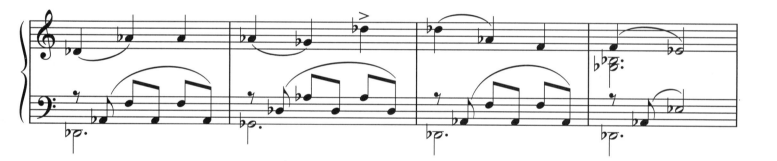

VOLDEMORT

Music by
JOHN WILLIAMS

Sinister ♩ = 69

Voldemort - 3 - 2
0639B